AF481154

ADDITION PRACTICE FOR 1ST GRADE LEARNERS

Math Books for 1st Graders
Children's Math Books

Hi Kids!

Lets practice addition.

Add the shapes to find the sum in each equation.

1)

__4__ + __3__ = __7__

2)

__1__ + __6__ = ____

3)

__10__ + __6__ = ____

4)

__9__ + __6__ = ____

5)

__1__ + __3__ = ____

6)

__6__ + __2__ = ____

EXERCISE NO. 2

Add the shapes to find the sum in each equation.

1)

___ 8 ___ + ___ 8 ___ = ______

2)

___ 10 ___ + ___ 5 ___ = ______

3)

___ 6 ___ + ___ 4 ___ = ______

4)

___ 7 ___ + ___ 10 ___ = ______

5)

___ 4 ___ + ___ 2 ___ = ______

6)

___ 6 ___ + ___ 3 ___ = ______

Add the shapes to find the sum in each equation.

1)

$+$

$\underline{\quad 3 \quad} + \underline{\quad 1 \quad} = \underline{\qquad}$

2)

$+$

$\underline{\quad 4 \quad} + \underline{\quad 5 \quad} = \underline{\qquad}$

3)

$+$

$\underline{\quad 5 \quad} + \underline{\quad 5 \quad} = \underline{\qquad}$

4)

$+$

$\underline{\quad 3 \quad} + \underline{\quad 6 \quad} = \underline{\qquad}$

5)

$+$

$\underline{\quad 3 \quad} + \underline{\quad 3 \quad} = \underline{\qquad}$

6)

$+$

$\underline{\quad 2 \quad} + \underline{\quad 3 \quad} = \underline{\qquad}$

Add the shapes to find the sum in each equation.

1)

$\underline{\quad 4 \quad} + \underline{\quad 6 \quad} = \underline{\qquad}$

2)

$\underline{\quad 2 \quad} + \underline{\quad 7 \quad} = \underline{\qquad}$

3)

$\underline{\quad 6 \quad} + \underline{\quad 10 \quad} = \underline{\qquad}$

4)

$\underline{\quad 6 \quad} + \underline{\quad 1 \quad} = \underline{\qquad}$

5)

$\underline{\quad 7 \quad} + \underline{\quad 4 \quad} = \underline{\qquad}$

6)

$\underline{\quad 9 \quad} + \underline{\quad 4 \quad} = \underline{\qquad}$

Add the shapes to find the sum in each equation.

1)

$9 + 4 =$ ____

2)

$6 + 6 =$ ____

3)

$3 + 8 =$ ____

4)

$1 + 4 =$ ____

5)

$4 + 10 =$ ____

6)

$5 + 9 =$ ____

Add the shapes to find the sum in each equation.

1) _5_ + _6_ = ____

2) _3_ + _1_ = ____

3) _9_ + _4_ = ____

4) _8_ + _9_ = ____

5) _2_ + _3_ = ____

6) _5_ + _7_ = ____

EXERCISE NO. 7

Add the shapes to find the sum in each equation.

1) ⬡⬡⬡⬡⬡⬡⬡⬡⬡⬡
   + ⬡⬡⬡
   ____

   10 + 3 = ____

2) ♡♡♡♡♡♡
   + ♡♡♡♡♡♡♡♡♡
   ____

   6 + 9 = ____

3) △△△△△△△△△△
   + △
   ____

   10 + 1 = ____

4) ◇
   + ◇◇◇◇◇◇
   ____

   1 + 6 = ____

5) ■■■■
   + ■■■■■
   ____

   4 + 5 = ____

6) ⬡⬡⬡
   + ⬡⬡⬡⬡⬡⬡⬡
   ____

   3 + 7 = ____

Add the shapes to find the sum in each equation.

1)

$\underline{\quad 1 \quad} + \underline{\quad 3 \quad} = \underline{\qquad}$

2)

$\underline{\quad 6 \quad} + \underline{\quad 3 \quad} = \underline{\qquad}$

3)

$\underline{\quad 9 \quad} + \underline{\quad 5 \quad} = \underline{\qquad}$

4)

$\underline{\quad 6 \quad} + \underline{\quad 2 \quad} = \underline{\qquad}$

5)

$\underline{\quad 1 \quad} + \underline{\quad 4 \quad} = \underline{\qquad}$

6)

$\underline{\quad 7 \quad} + \underline{\quad 4 \quad} = \underline{\qquad}$

Add the shapes to find the sum in each equation.

1)

6 + 10 = ______

2)

3 + 5 = ______

3)

3 + 9 = ______

4)

9 + 2 = ______

5)

8 + 4 = ______

6)

10 + 4 = ______

Add the shapes to find the sum in each equation.

1) __8__ + __2__ = _____

2) __9__ + __8__ = _____

3) __1__ + __10__ = _____

4) __6__ + __8__ = _____

5) __4__ + __10__ = _____

6) __7__ + __1__ = _____

EXERCISE NO. 11

Find the sum in each equation.

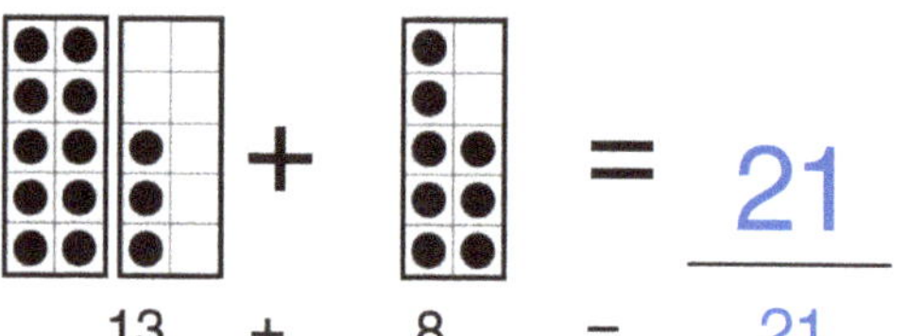

13 + 8 = 21

21

14 + 17 = _____

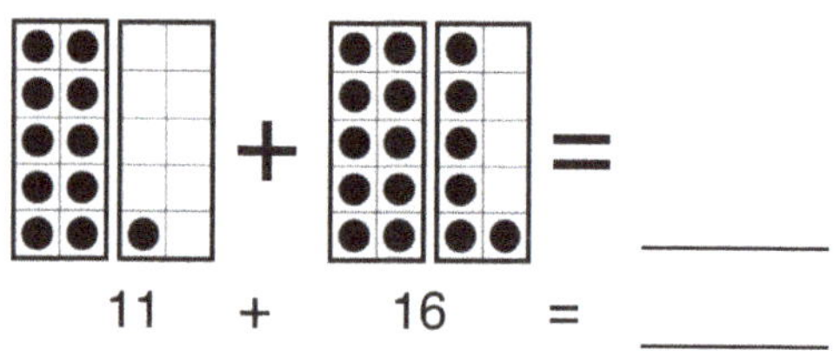

11 + 16 = _____

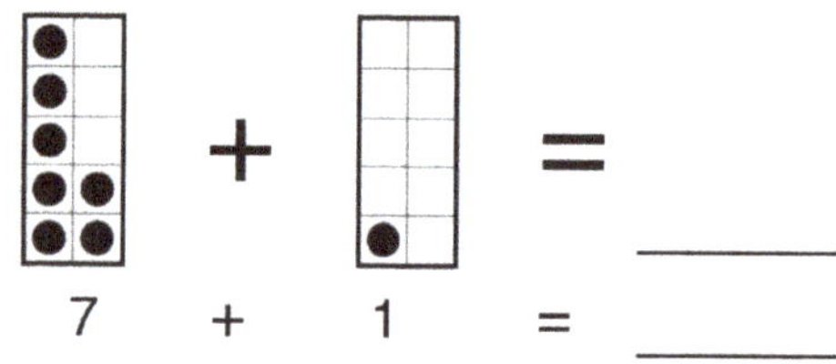

7 + 1 = _____

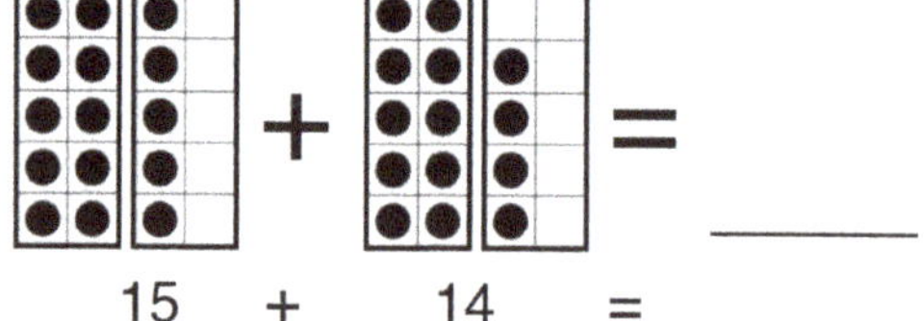

15 + 14 = _____

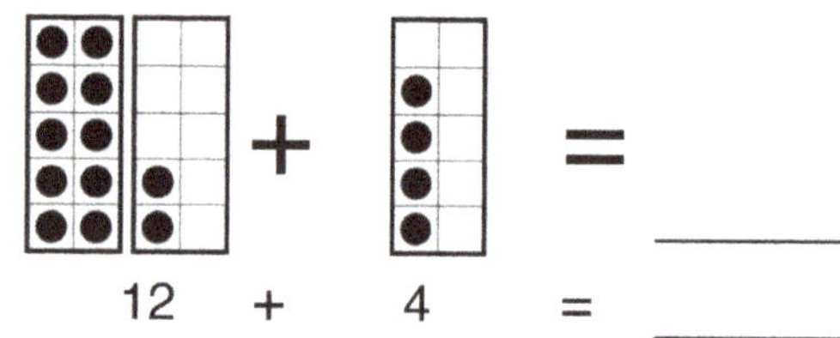

12 + 4 = _____

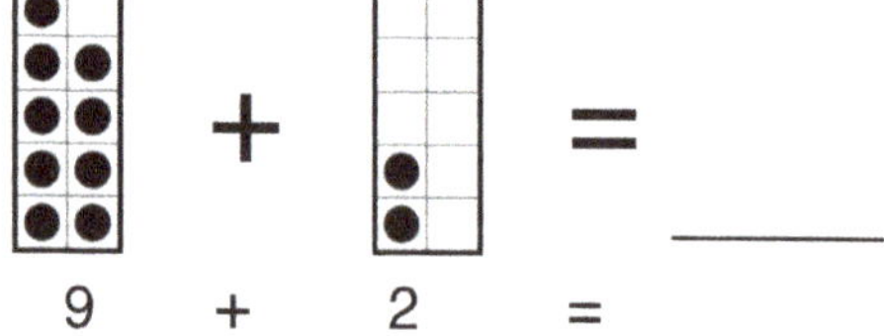

9 + 2 = _____

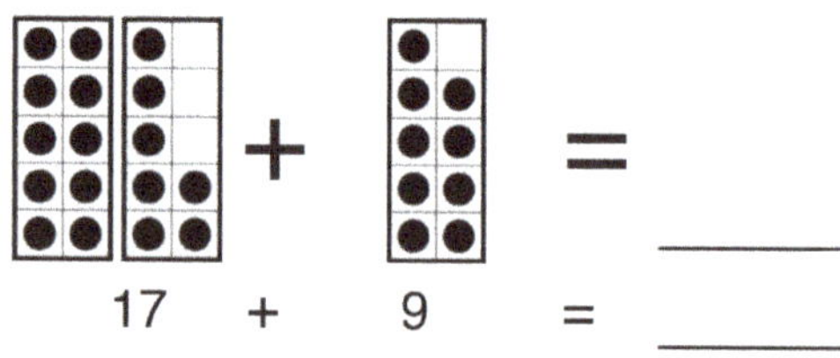

17 + 9 = _____

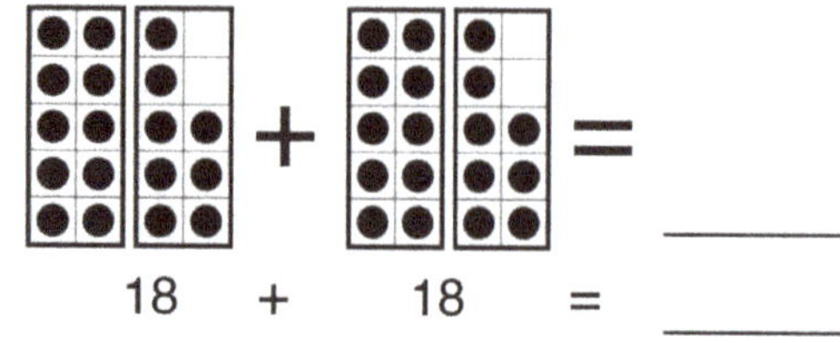

8 + 6 = _____

18 + 18 = _____

Find the sum in each equation.

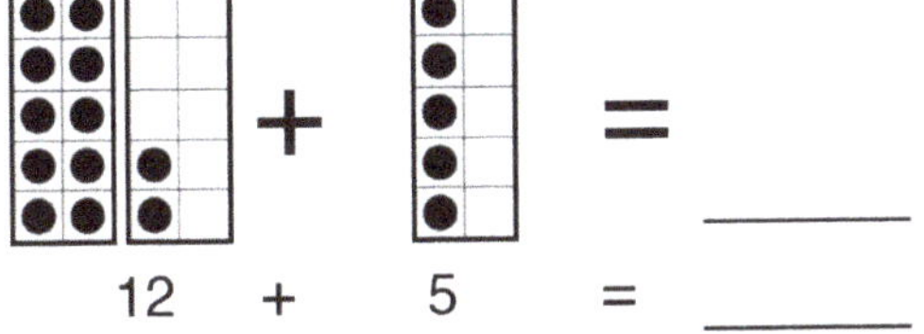

20 + 9 = ______

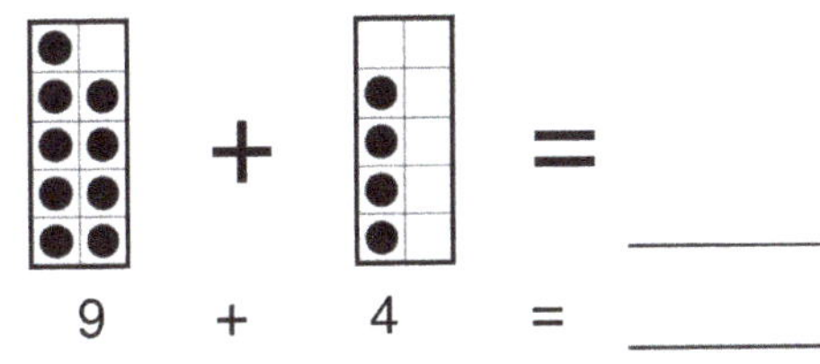

7 + 6 = ______

6 + 16 = ______

10 + 7 = ______

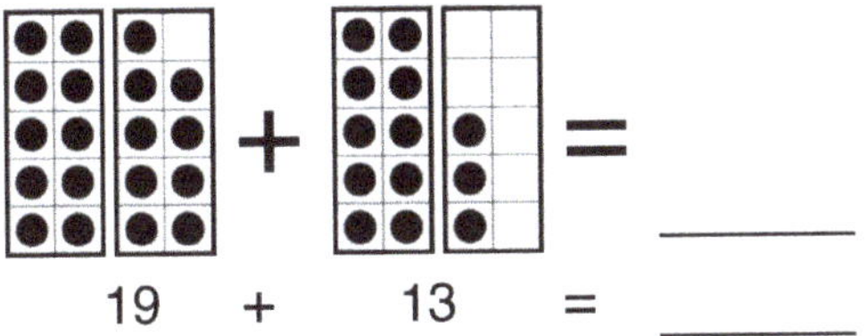

12 + 5 = ______

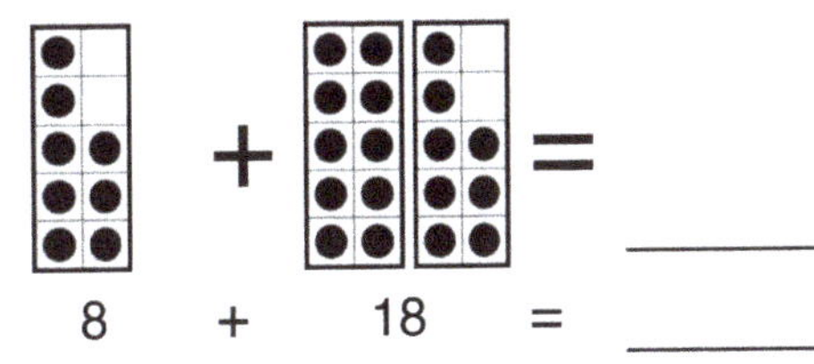

9 + 4 = ______

19 + 13 = ______

8 + 18 = ______

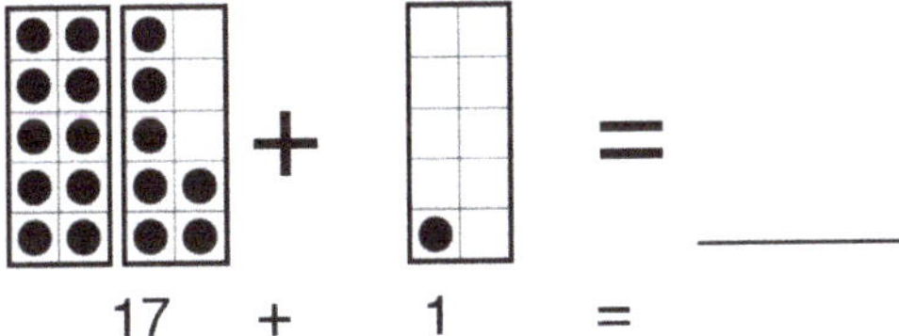

17 + 1 = ______

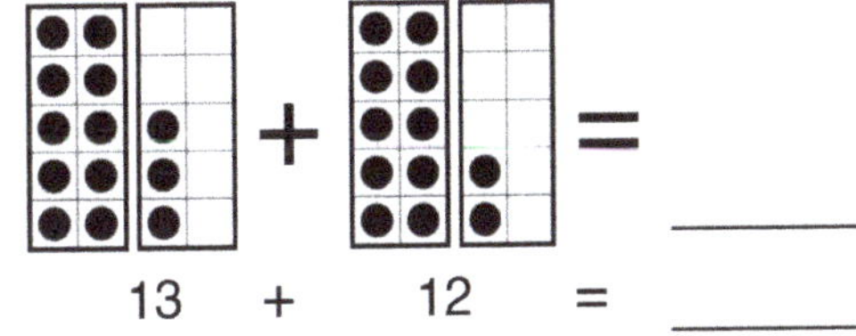

13 + 12 = ______

EXERCISE NO. 13

Find the sum in each equation.

10 + 18 = ______

19 + 2 = ______

6 + 14 = ______

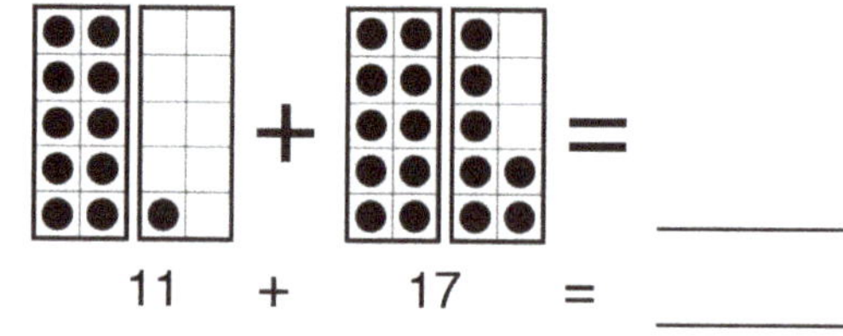

11 + 17 = ______

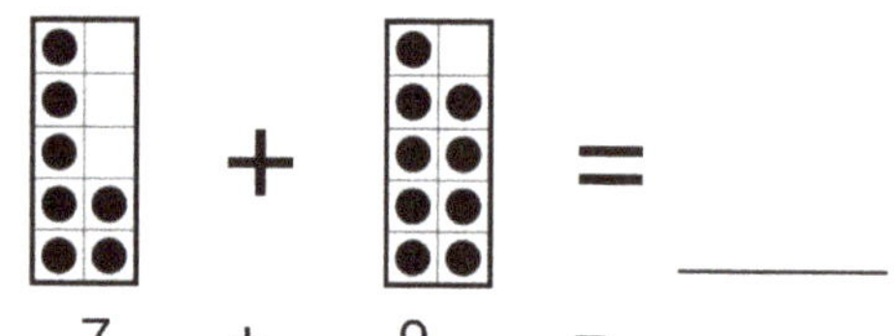

7 + 9 = ______

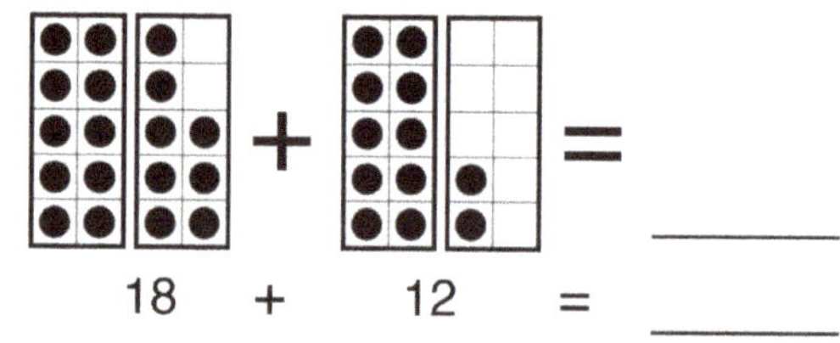

18 + 12 = ______

20 + 19 = ______

12 + 6 = ______

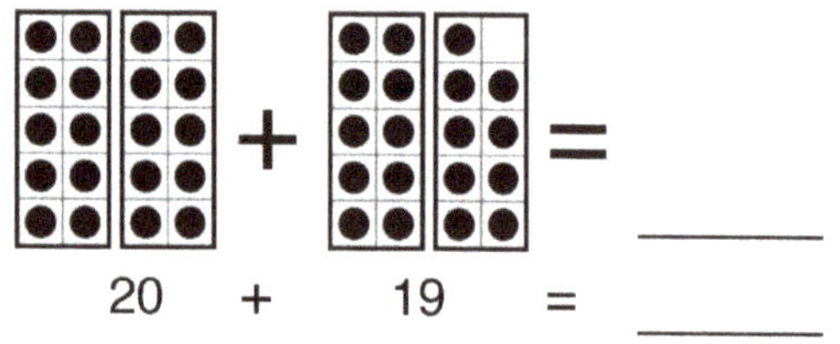

16 + 3 = ______

8 + 8 = ______

Find the sum in each equation.

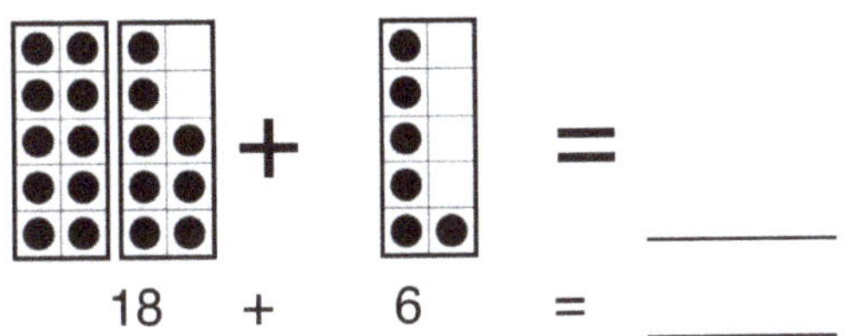

12 + 3 = _____

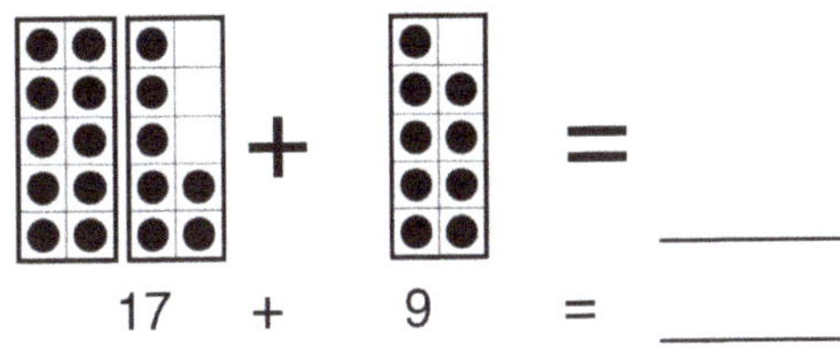

16 + 13 = _____

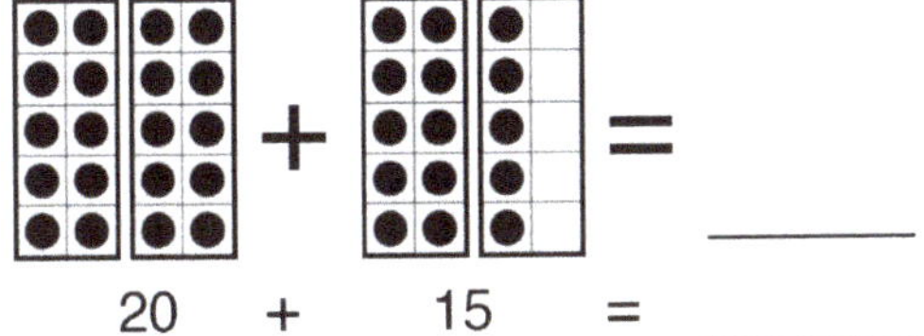

18 + 6 = _____

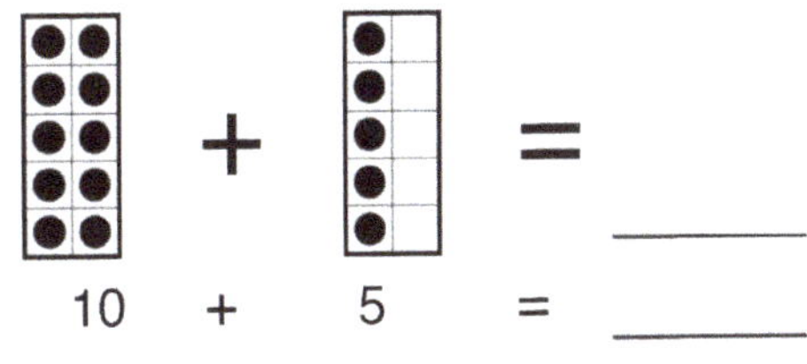

17 + 9 = _____

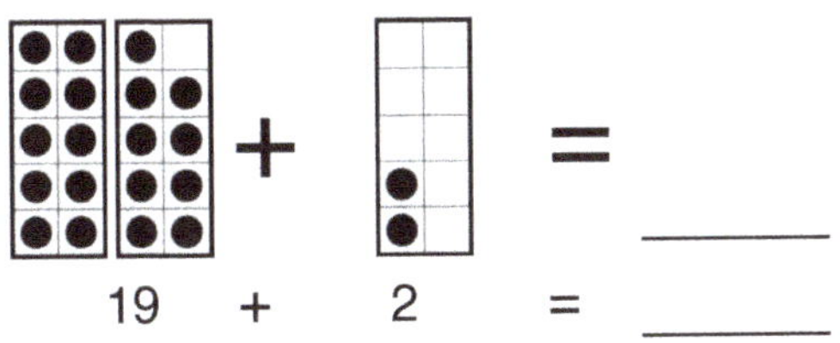

20 + 15 = _____

10 + 5 = _____

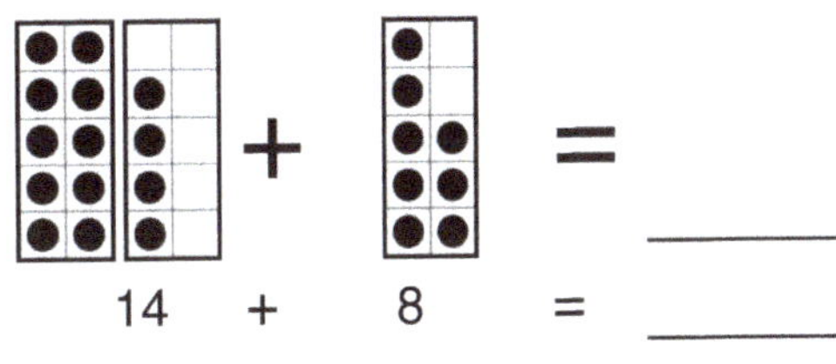

19 + 2 = _____

14 + 8 = _____

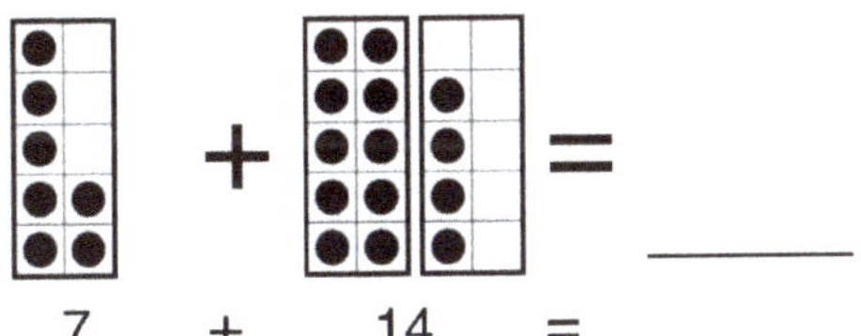

7 + 14 = _____

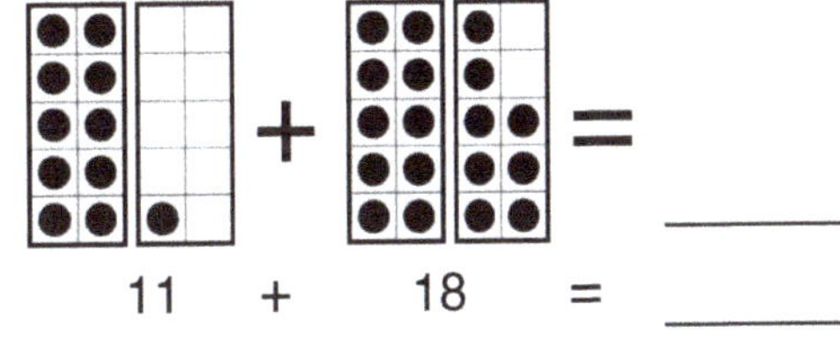

11 + 18 = _____

Find the sum in each equation.

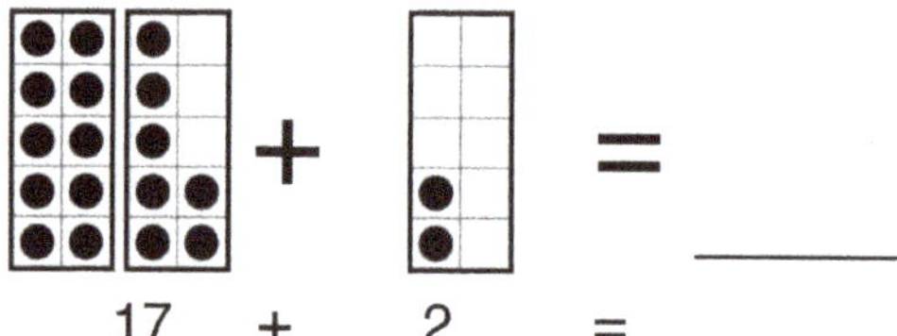

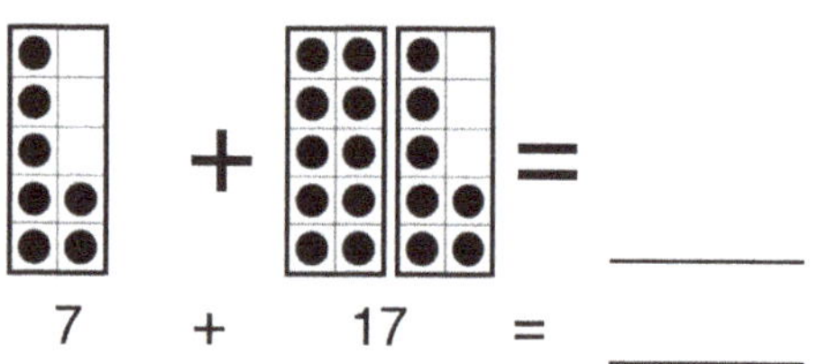
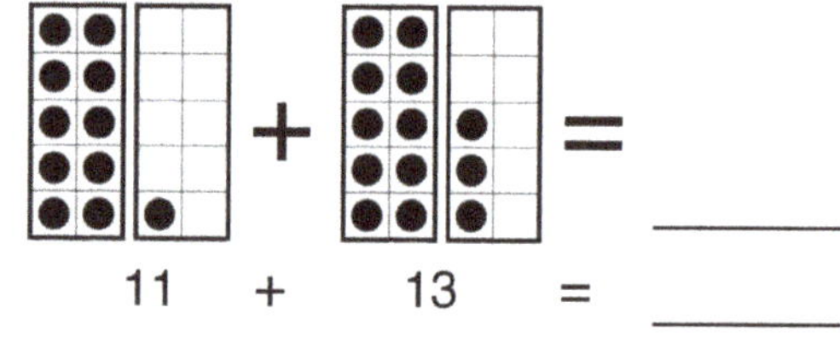

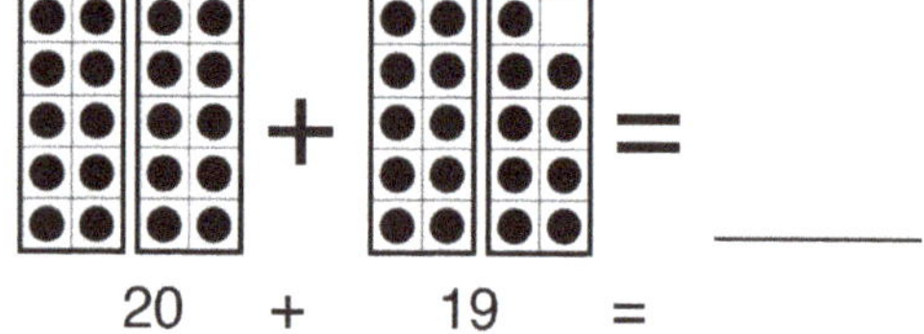
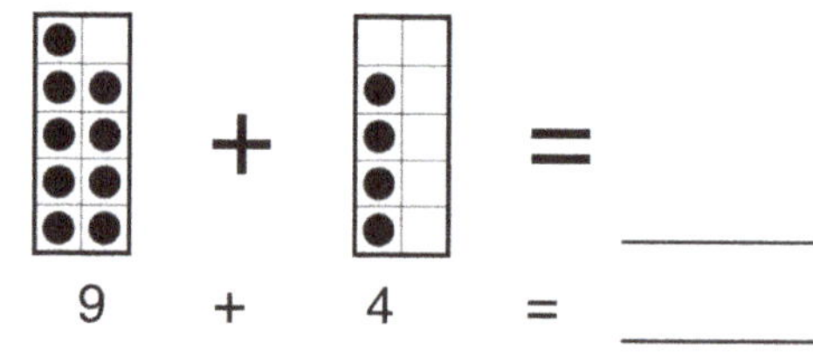

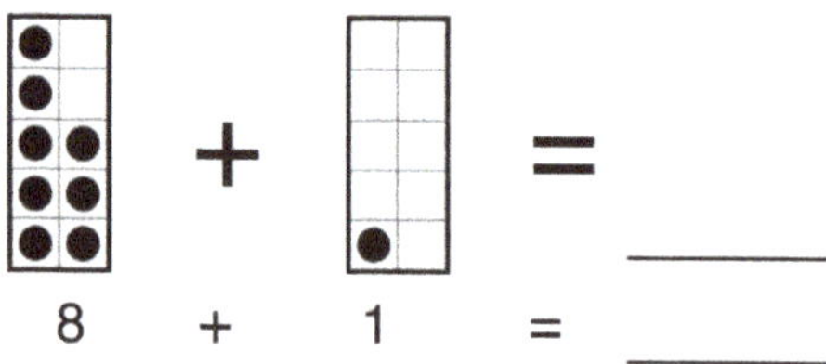
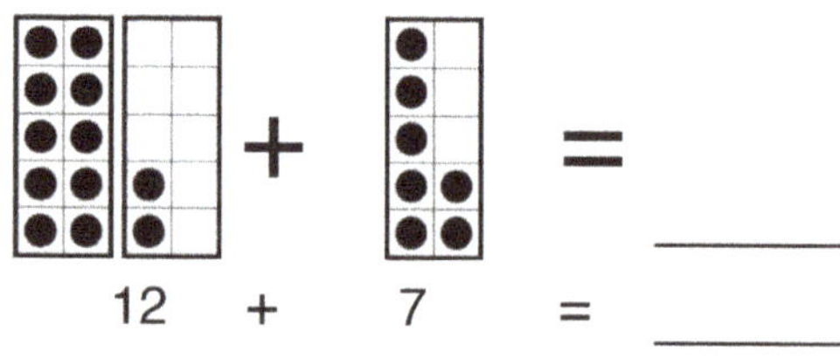

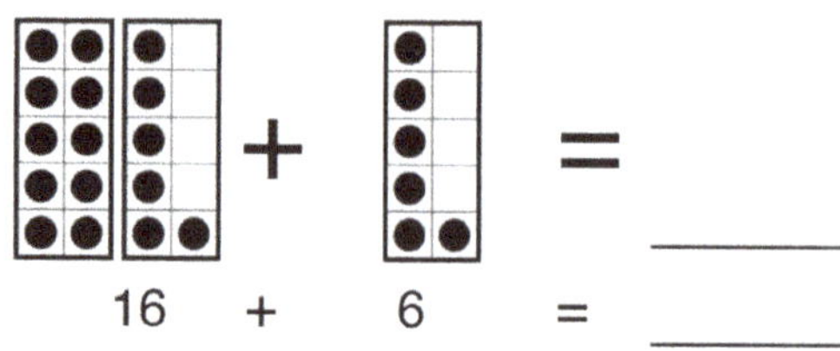

EXERCISE NO. 16

Find the sum in each equation.

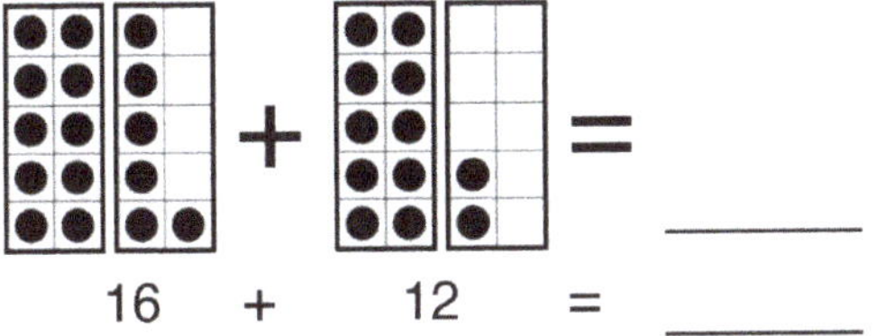

20 + 9 = _____   7 + 19 = _____

17 + 5 = _____   11 + 18 = _____

16 + 12 = _____   6 + 7 = _____

9 + 4 = _____   8 + 16 = _____

10 + 15 = _____   19 + 13 = _____

Find the sum in each equation.

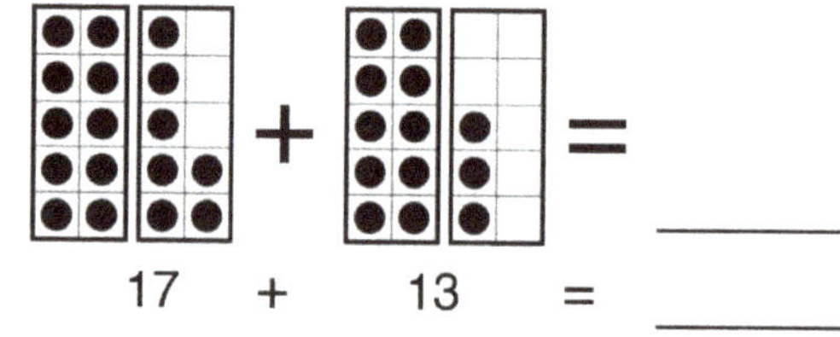

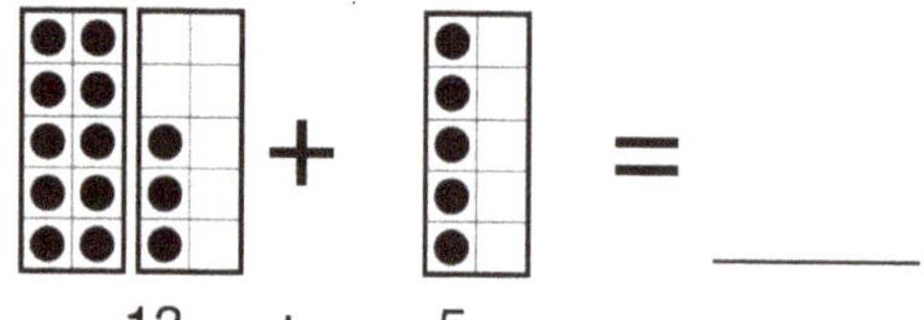

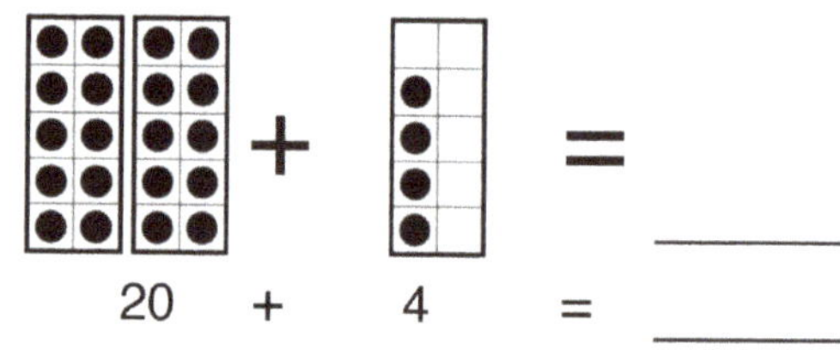

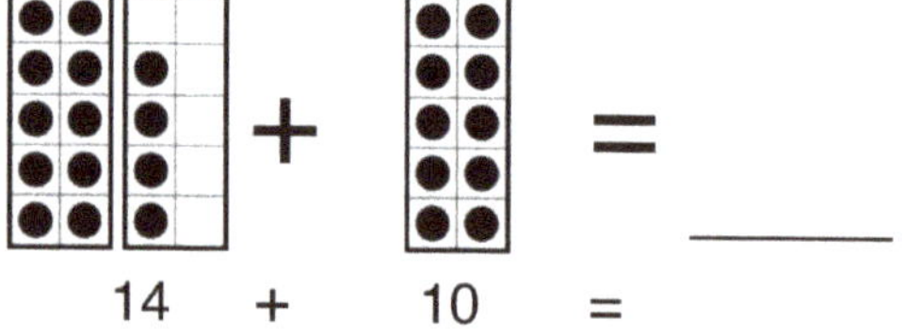

9 + 15 = _____

12 + 18 = _____

8 + 2 = _____

17 + 13 = _____

13 + 5 = _____

20 + 4 = _____

14 + 10 = _____

15 + 1 = _____

18 + 9 = _____

19 + 6 = _____

EXERCISE NO. 18

Find the sum in each equation.

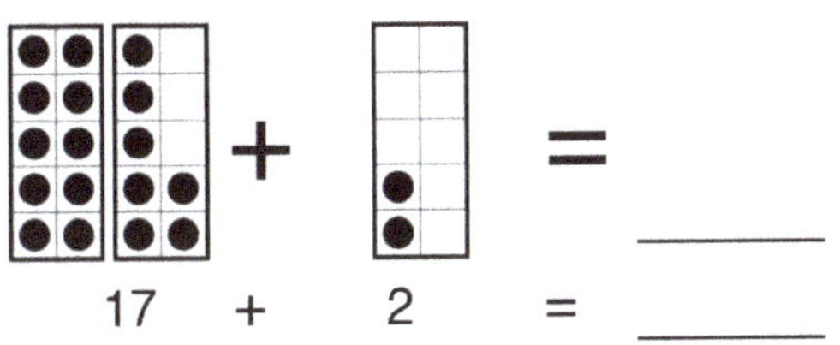

11 + 13 = _____

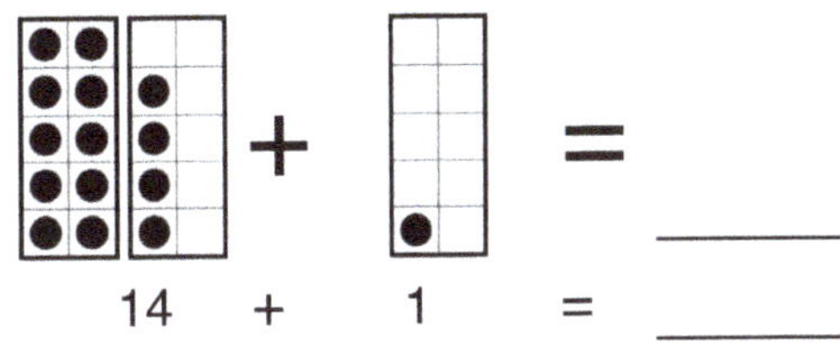

12 + 8 = _____

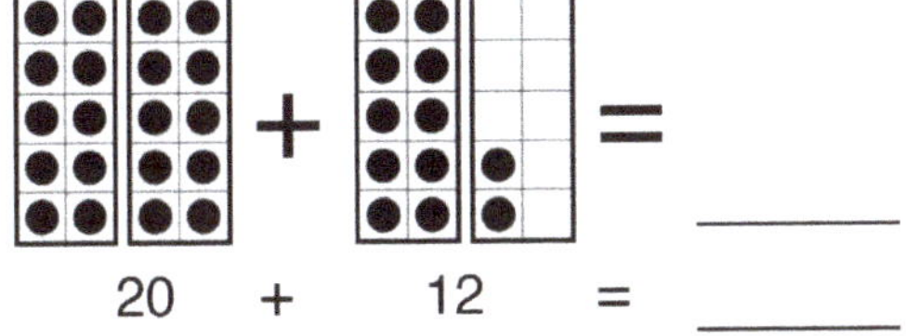

17 + 2 = _____

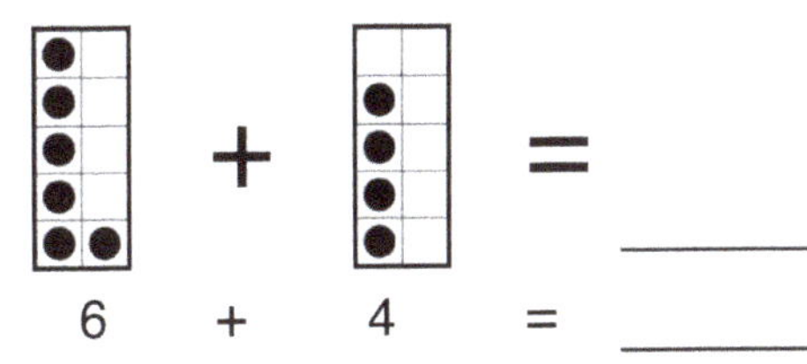

14 + 1 = _____

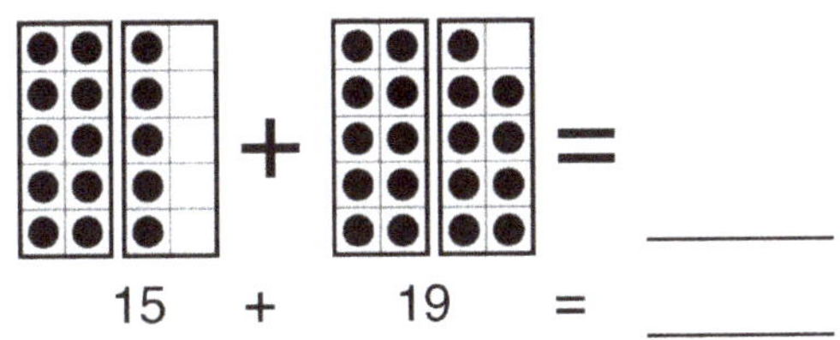

20 + 12 = _____

6 + 4 = _____

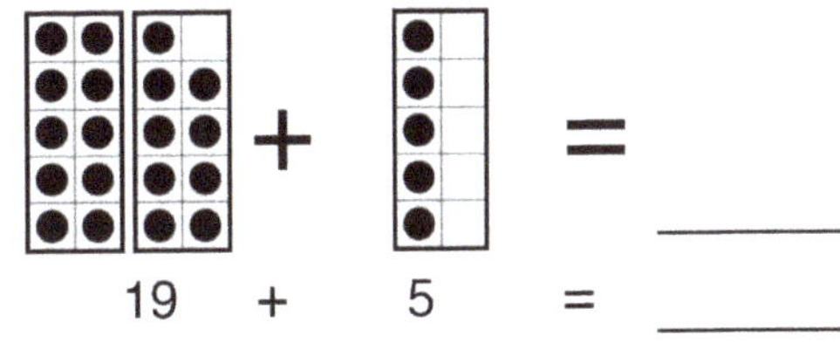

15 + 19 = _____

19 + 5 = _____

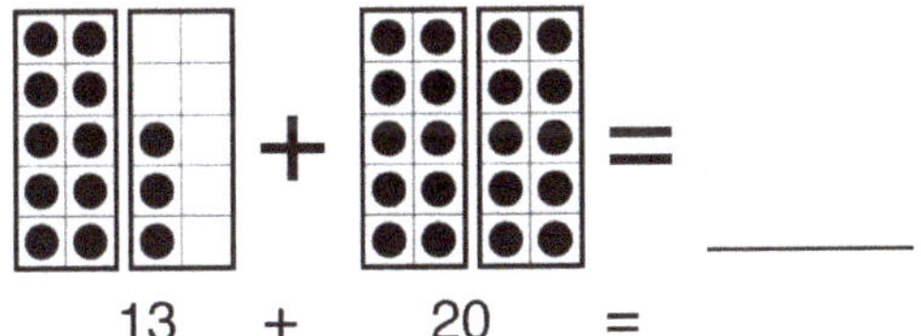

13 + 20 = _____

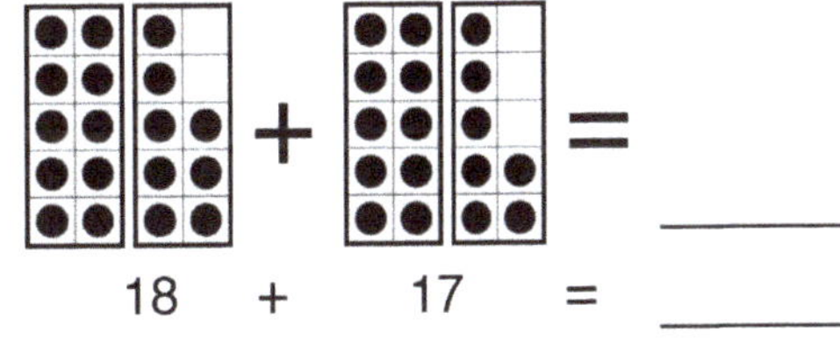

18 + 17 = _____

Find the sum in each equation.

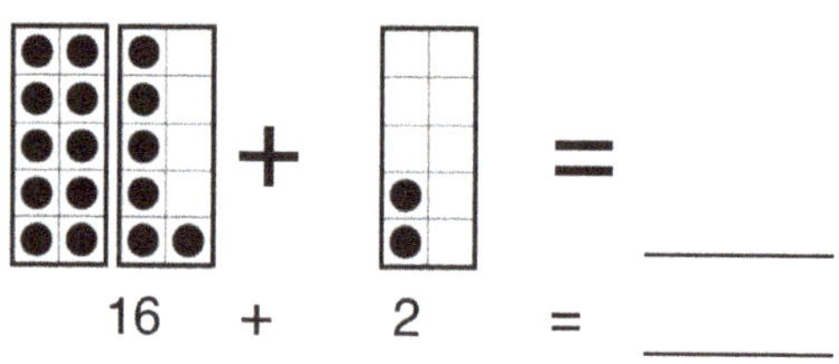

19 + 16 = _____

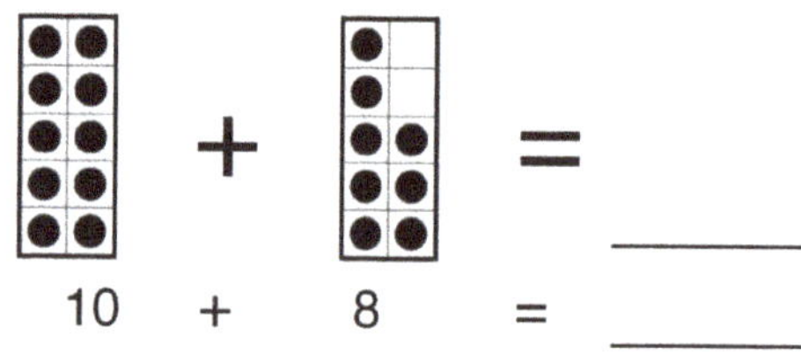

18 + 17 = _____

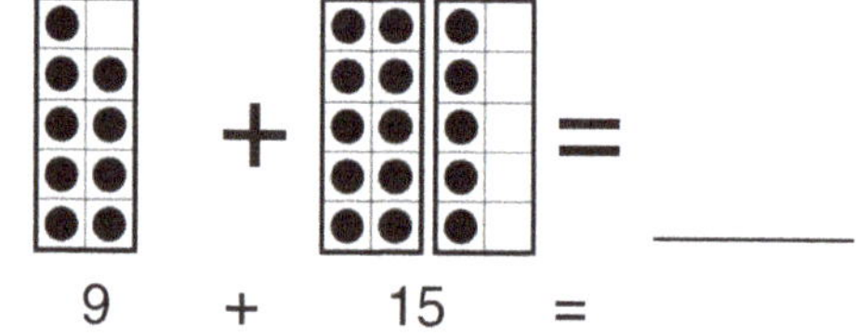

16 + 2 = _____

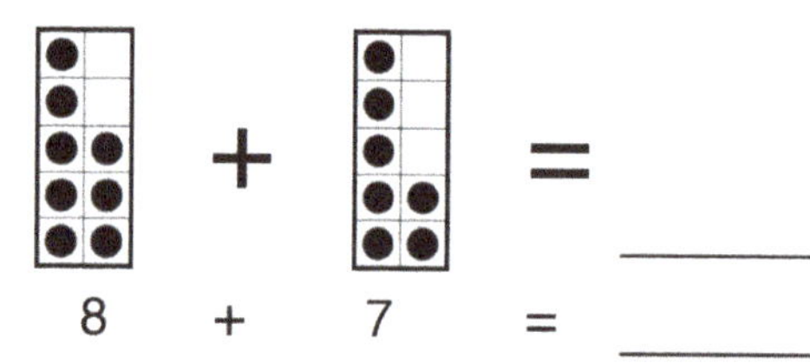

10 + 8 = _____

9 + 15 = _____

8 + 7 = _____

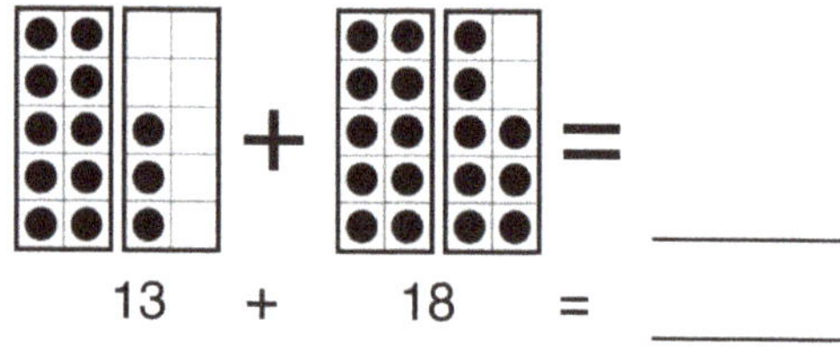

13 + 18 = _____

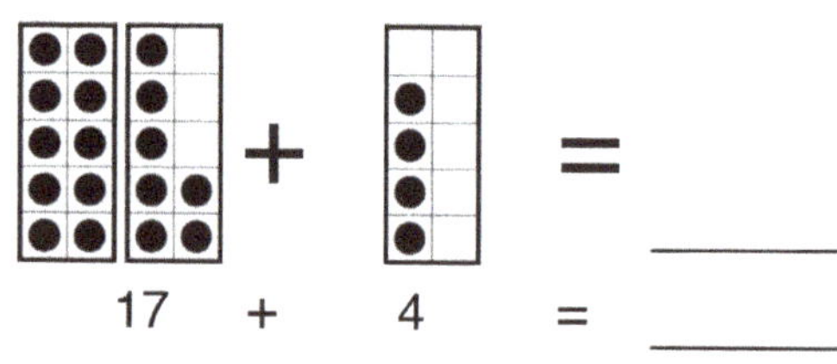

17 + 4 = _____

20 + 11 = _____

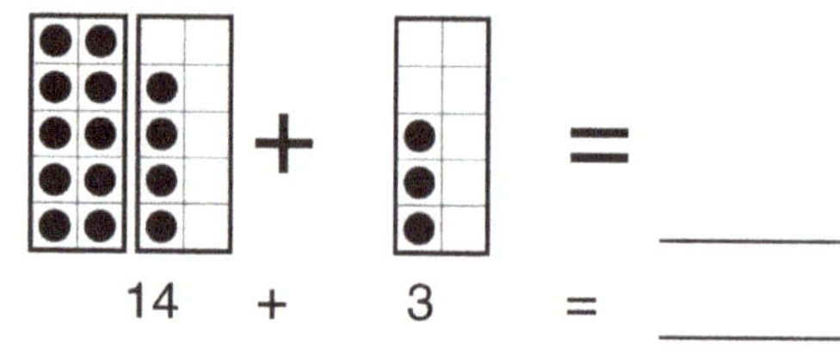

14 + 3 = _____

Find the sum in each equation.

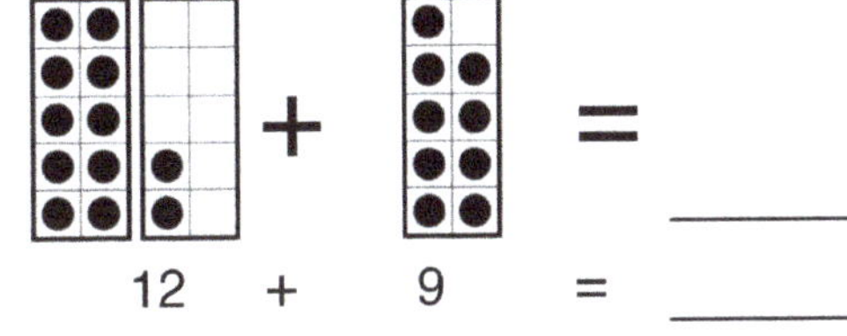

13 + 20 = ____

18 + 15 = ____

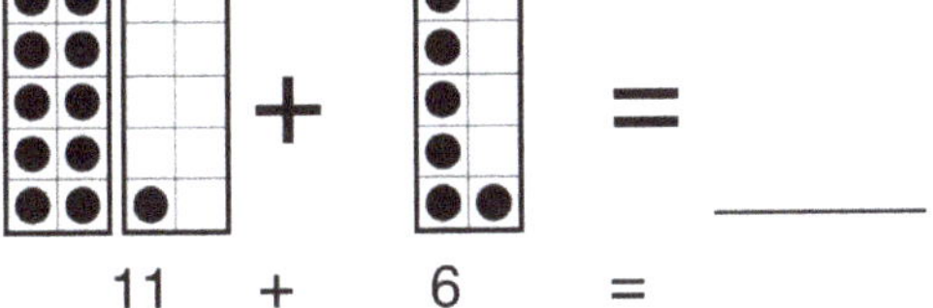
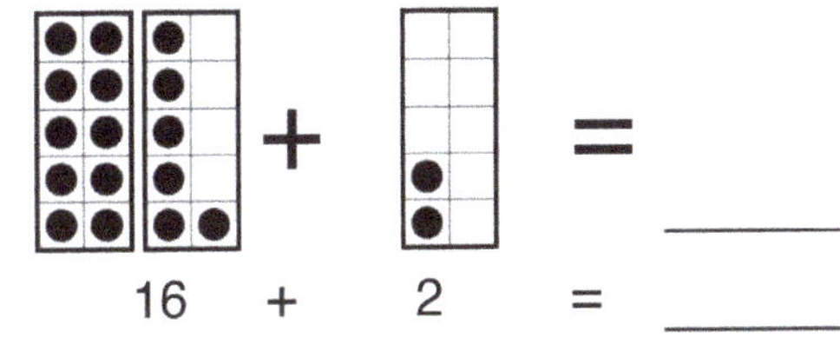

17 + 11 = ____

12 + 9 = ____

11 + 6 = ____

16 + 2 = ____

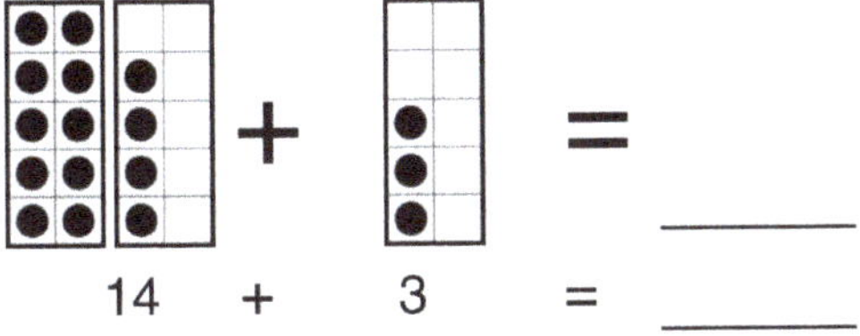
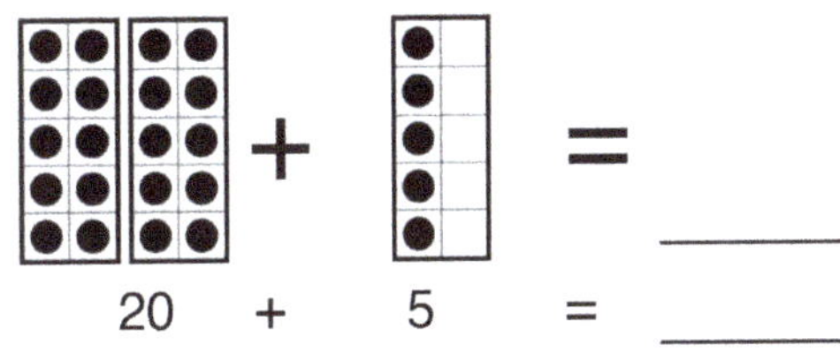

14 + 3 = ____

20 + 5 = ____

10 + 18 = ____

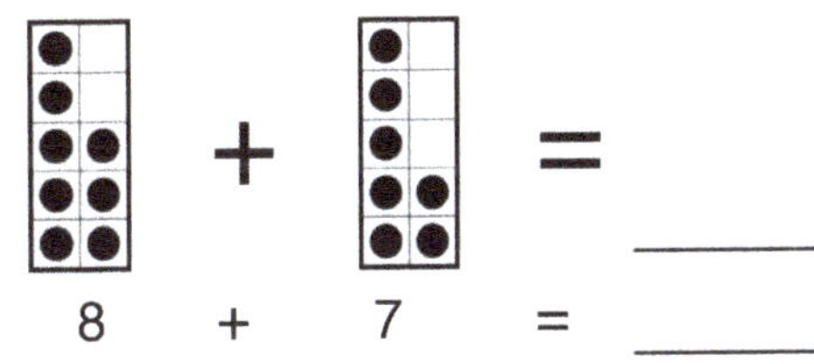

8 + 7 = ____

Find the sum in each equation.

8 + 9 17	6 + 6	2 + 1	5 + 0
6 + 5	2 + 5	5 + 4	7 + 0
9 + 7	9 + 3	2 + 4	5 + 6

Find the sum in each equation.

4 + 4	1 + 4	3 + 7	6 + 5
2 + 4	9 + 0	1 + 3	6 + 0
7 + 3	7 + 8	7 + 8	9 + 4

Find the sum in each equation.

6 +7	6 +2	3 +5	8 +8
3 +2	2 +8	3 +7	8 +3
9 +9	2 +0	9 +3	7 +3

Find the sum in each equation.

1 + 4	3 + 7	7 + 7	4 + 3
8 + 6	9 + 5	9 + 9	6 + 5
8 + 4	6 + 6	5 + 5	1 + 9

Find the sum in each equation.

3 + 7	1 + 0	6 + 6	5 + 7
7 + 5	6 + 4	2 + 5	3 + 2
5 + 5	1 + 8	7 + 9	5 + 5

Find the sum in each equation.

4 + 6	1 + 1	5 + 6	6 + 5
6 + 2	4 + 3	6 + 0	2 + 5
9 + 9	9 + 6	6 + 2	0 + 4

EXERCISE NO. 27

Find the sum in each equation.

8 + 2	5 + 6	1 + 4	4 + 8
1 + 6	5 + 9	2 + 8	1 + 7
9 + 6	2 + 8	1 + 6	5 + 5

Find the sum in each equation.

$$12 + 3$$
$$14 + 8$$
$$16 + 6$$
$$19 + 9$$

$$14 + 2$$
$$9 + 6$$
$$18 + 1$$
$$15 + 9$$

$$13 + 7$$
$$12 + 4$$
$$16 + 4$$
$$19 + 1$$

Find the sum in each equation.

$14 + 1$	$18 + 5$	$17 + 8$	$16 + 7$
$12 + 8$	$9 + 4$	$17 + 7$	$15 + 3$
$19 + 9$	$13 + 1$	$18 + 5$	$16 + 6$

Find the sum in each equation.

9	10	11	13
+ 3	+ 7	+ 3	+ 8

14	16	15	10
+ 5	+ 2	+ 2	+ 9

12	14	17	11
+ 1	+ 6	+ 5	+ 1

Find the sum in each equation.

```
    9         16         10         18
 +  8      +   7      +   3      +   6
```

```
   19         13         15         12
 +  6      +   1      +   1      +   5
```

```
   14         11         14         18
 +  4      +   3      +   5      +   2
```

Find the sum in each equation.

18 + 9	17 + 3	16 + 5	11 + 4
13 + 6	12 + 5	16 + 6	17 + 4
13 + 2	9 + 1	11 + 1	19 + 2

Find the sum in each equation.

16	11	13	15
+ 8	+ 6	+ 6	+ 1

19	17	9	9
+ 7	+ 7	+ 9	+ 4

12	16	10	13
+ 9	+ 8	+ 4	+ 3

EXERCISE NO. 34

Find the sum in each equation.

9 + 1	15 + 1	16 + 7	10 + 7
17 + 8	19 + 3	12 + 6	13 + 4
17 + 9	10 + 5	12 + 3	11 + 5

Find the sum in each equation.

| 13 | 11 | 12 | 9 |
| + 3 | + 2 | + 9 | + 9 |

| 15 | 10 | 16 | 17 |
| + 7 | + 4 | + 5 | + 4 |

| 19 | 12 | 15 | 14 |
| + 7 | + 1 | + 5 | + 2 |

Find the sum in each equation.

9 + 9	17 + 9	15 + 2	17 + 4
15 + 3	19 + 3	18 + 6	13 + 8
9 + 2	16 + 5	11 + 7	13 + 1

Find the sum in each equation.

13 + 4	17 + 8	9 + 3	9 + 9
18 + 8	14 + 2	10 + 4	19 + 7
16 + 6	14 + 9	12 + 1	19 + 1

Find the sum in each equation.

13 + 9	11 + 4	10 + 1	17 + 8
18 + 7	15 + 2	9 + 5	13 + 5
19 + 3	12 + 6	12 + 7	18 + 1

EXERCISE NO. 39

Find the sum in each equation.

20 + 11	11 + 15	18 + 20	12 + 16
15 + 13	19 + 15	17 + 14	15 + 10
18 + 14	12 + 12	14 + 13	17 + 11

Find the sum in each equation.

17 + 18	18 + 20	15 + 14	18 + 16
15 + 13	11 + 16	17 + 17	14 + 10
13 + 15	10 + 17	13 + 19	20 + 20

Find the sum in each equation.

14 + 11	10 + 10	12 + 11	19 + 13
18 + 12	15 + 20	11 + 19	13 + 15
10 + 16	17 + 14	16 + 14	20 + 17

Find the sum in each equation.

$$\begin{array}{r} 17 \\ +13 \\ \hline \end{array} \qquad \begin{array}{r} 13 \\ +12 \\ \hline \end{array} \qquad \begin{array}{r} 11 \\ +19 \\ \hline \end{array} \qquad \begin{array}{r} 10 \\ +19 \\ \hline \end{array}$$

$$\begin{array}{r} 16 \\ +13 \\ \hline \end{array} \qquad \begin{array}{r} 20 \\ +10 \\ \hline \end{array} \qquad \begin{array}{r} 11 \\ +18 \\ \hline \end{array} \qquad \begin{array}{r} 12 \\ +17 \\ \hline \end{array}$$

$$\begin{array}{r} 20 \\ +10 \\ \hline \end{array} \qquad \begin{array}{r} 19 \\ +11 \\ \hline \end{array} \qquad \begin{array}{r} 18 \\ +17 \\ \hline \end{array} \qquad \begin{array}{r} 17 \\ +16 \\ \hline \end{array}$$

Find the sum in each equation.

19 + 10	12 + 13	10 + 12	14 + 19
13 + 15	18 + 16	20 + 14	17 + 15
15 + 13	19 + 10	18 + 20	12 + 17

Find the sum in each equation.

20 + 18	13 + 20	12 + 20	17 + 14
16 + 17	13 + 13	10 + 13	18 + 12
10 + 16	14 + 10	19 + 19	15 + 12

Find the sum in each equation.

14 + 10	15 + 19	10 + 14	14 + 20
16 + 17	19 + 18	17 + 14	16 + 16
15 + 12	10 + 10	13 + 17	19 + 13

Find the sum in each equation.

17 + 12	13 + 13	15 + 20	11 + 18
18 + 16	14 + 11	15 + 17	12 + 11
17 + 13	12 + 10	11 + 15	10 + 19

EXERCISE NO. 1	EXERCISE NO. 2

EXERCISE NO. 1

1) $4 + 3 = 7$

2) $1 + 6 = 7$

3) $10 + 6 = 16$

4) $9 + 6 = 15$

5) $1 + 3 = 4$

6) $6 + 2 = 8$

EXERCISE NO. 2

1) $8 + 8 = 16$

2) $10 + 5 = 15$

3) $6 + 4 = 10$

4) $7 + 10 = 17$

5) $4 + 2 = 6$

6) $6 + 3 = 9$

EXERCISE NO. 3

1) $\underline{\ 3\ } + \underline{\ 1\ } = \underline{\ 4\ }$

2) $\underline{\ 4\ } + \underline{\ 5\ } = \underline{\ 9\ }$

3) $\underline{\ 5\ } + \underline{\ 5\ } = \underline{\ 10\ }$

4) $\underline{\ 3\ } + \underline{\ 6\ } = \underline{\ 9\ }$

5) $\underline{\ 3\ } + \underline{\ 3\ } = \underline{\ 6\ }$

6) $\underline{\ 2\ } + \underline{\ 3\ } = \underline{\ 5\ }$

EXERCISE NO. 4

1) $\underline{\ 4\ } + \underline{\ 6\ } = \underline{\ 10\ }$

2) $\underline{\ 2\ } + \underline{\ 7\ } = \underline{\ 9\ }$

3) $\underline{\ 6\ } + \underline{\ 10\ } = \underline{\ 16\ }$

4) $\underline{\ 6\ } + \underline{\ 1\ } = \underline{\ 7\ }$

5) $\underline{\ 7\ } + \underline{\ 4\ } = \underline{\ 11\ }$

6) $\underline{\ 9\ } + \underline{\ 4\ } = \underline{\ 13\ }$

EXERCISE NO. 5

1) $\underline{\ 9\ } + \underline{\ 4\ } = \underline{\ 13\ }$

2) $\underline{\ 6\ } + \underline{\ 6\ } = \underline{\ 12\ }$

3) $\underline{\ 3\ } + \underline{\ 8\ } = \underline{\ 11\ }$

4) $\underline{\ 1\ } + \underline{\ 4\ } = \underline{\ 5\ }$

5) $\underline{\ 4\ } + \underline{\ 10\ } = \underline{\ 14\ }$

6) $\underline{\ 5\ } + \underline{\ 9\ } = \underline{\ 14\ }$

EXERCISE NO. 6

1) $\underline{\ 5\ } + \underline{\ 6\ } = \underline{\ 11\ }$

2) $\underline{\ 3\ } + \underline{\ 1\ } = \underline{\ 4\ }$

3) $\underline{\ 9\ } + \underline{\ 4\ } = \underline{\ 13\ }$

4) $\underline{\ 8\ } + \underline{\ 9\ } = \underline{\ 17\ }$

5) $\underline{\ 2\ } + \underline{\ 3\ } = \underline{\ 5\ }$

6) $\underline{\ 5\ } + \underline{\ 7\ } = \underline{\ 12\ }$

EXERCISE NO. 7

1) 10 + 3 = 13

2) 6 + 9 = 15

3) 10 + 1 = 11

4) 1 + 6 = 7

5) 4 + 5 = 9

6) 3 + 7 = 10

EXERCISE NO. 8

1) 1 + 3 = 4

2) 6 + 3 = 9

3) 9 + 5 = 14

4) 6 + 2 = 8

5) 1 + 4 = 5

6) 7 + 4 = 11

EXERCISE NO. 9

1) 6 + 10 = 16

2) 3 + 5 = 8

3) 3 + 9 = 12

4) 9 + 2 = 11

5) 8 + 4 = 12

6) 10 + 4 = 14

EXERCISE NO. 10

1) 8 + 2 = 10

2) 9 + 8 = 17

3) 1 + 10 = 11

4) 6 + 8 = 14

5) 4 + 10 = 14

6) 7 + 1 = 8

EXERCISE NO. 11

13 + 8 = **21**
13 + 8 = 21

14 + 17 = **31**
14 + 17 = 31

11 + 16 = **27**
11 + 16 = 27

7 + 1 = **8**
7 + 1 = 8

15 + 14 = **29**
15 + 14 = 29

12 + 4 = **16**
12 + 4 = 16

9 + 2 = **11**
9 + 2 = 11

17 + 9 = **26**
17 + 9 = 26

8 + 6 = **14**
8 + 6 = 14

18 + 18 = **36**
18 + 18 = 36

EXERCISE NO. 12

20 + 9 = **29**
20 + 9 = 29

7 + 6 = **13**
7 + 6 = 13

6 + 16 = **22**
6 + 16 = 22

10 + 7 = **17**
10 + 7 = 17

12 + 5 = **17**
12 + 5 = 17

9 + 4 = **13**
9 + 4 = 13

19 + 13 = **32**
19 + 13 = 32

8 + 18 = **26**
8 + 18 = 26

17 + 1 = **18**
17 + 1 = 18

13 + 12 = **25**
13 + 12 = 25

EXERCISE NO. 13

10 + 18 = **28**
10 + 18 = 28

19 + 2 = **21**
19 + 2 = 21

6 + 14 = **20**
6 + 14 = 20

11 + 17 = **28**
11 + 17 = 28

7 + 9 = **16**
7 + 9 = 16

18 + 12 = **30**
18 + 12 = 30

20 + 19 = **39**
20 + 19 = 39

12 + 6 = **18**
12 + 6 = 18

16 + 3 = **19**
16 + 3 = 19

8 + 8 = **16**
8 + 8 = 16

EXERCISE NO. 14

12 + 3 = **15**
12 + 3 = 15

16 + 13 = **29**
16 + 13 = 29

18 + 6 = **24**
18 + 6 = 24

17 + 9 = **26**
17 + 9 = 26

20 + 15 = **35**
20 + 15 = 35

10 + 5 = **15**
10 + 5 = 15

19 + 2 = **21**
19 + 2 = 21

14 + 8 = **22**
14 + 8 = 22

7 + 14 = **21**
7 + 14 = 21

11 + 18 = **29**
11 + 18 = 29

EXERCISE NO. 15

17 + 2 = 19

15 + 20 = 35

7 + 17 = 24

11 + 13 = 24

20 + 19 = 39

9 + 4 = 13

8 + 1 = 9

12 + 7 = 19

6 + 11 = 17

16 + 6 = 22

EXERCISE NO. 16

20 + 9 = 29

7 + 19 = 26

17 + 5 = 22

11 + 18 = 29

16 + 12 = 28

6 + 7 = 13

9 + 4 = 13

8 + 16 = 24

10 + 15 = 25

19 + 13 = 32

EXERCISE NO. 17

9 + 15 = 24

12 + 18 = 30

8 + 2 = 10

17 + 13 = 30

13 + 5 = 18

20 + 4 = 24

14 + 10 = 24

15 + 1 = 16

18 + 9 = 27

19 + 6 = 25

EXERCISE NO. 18

11 + 13 = 24

12 + 8 = 20

17 + 2 = 19

14 + 1 = 15

20 + 12 = 32

6 + 4 = 10

15 + 19 = 34

19 + 5 = 24

13 + 20 = 33

18 + 17 = 35

EXERCISE NO. 19

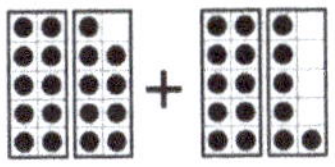

19 + 16 = **35**

18 + 17 = **35**

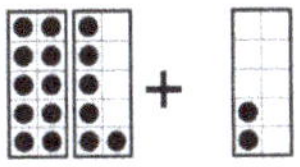

16 + 2 = **18**

10 + 8 = **18**

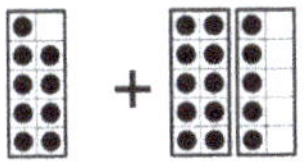

9 + 15 = **24**

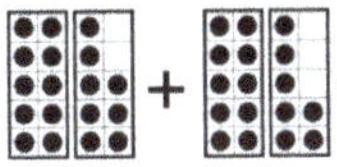

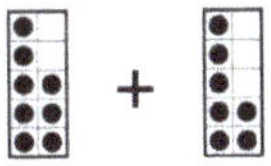

8 + 7 = **15**

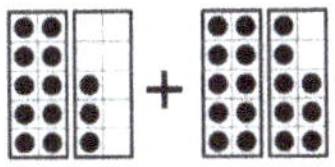

13 + 18 = **31**

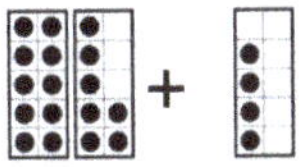

17 + 4 = **21**

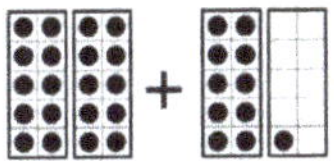

20 + 11 = **31**

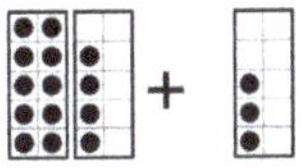

14 + 3 = **17**

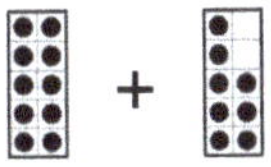

EXERCISE NO. 20

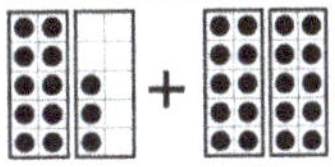

13 + 20 = **33**

18 + 15 = **33**

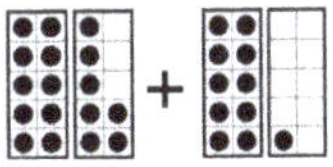

17 + 11 = **28**

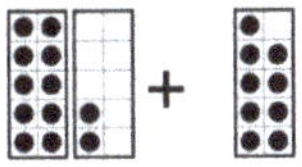

12 + 9 = **21**

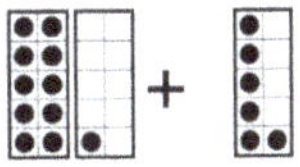

11 + 6 = **17**

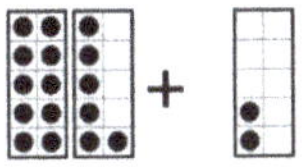

16 + 2 = **18**

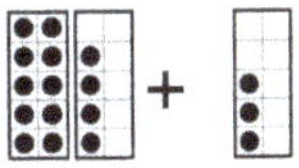

14 + 3 = **17**

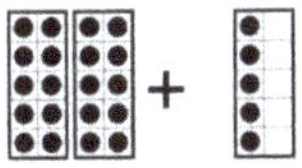

20 + 5 = **25**

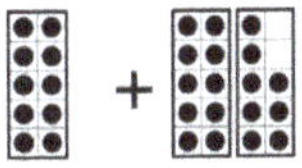

10 + 18 = **28**

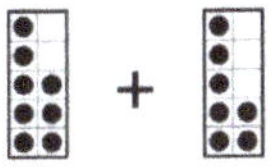

8 + 7 = **15**

EXERCISE NO. 21

$$\begin{array}{r} 8 \\ +\,9 \\ \hline 17 \end{array} \qquad \begin{array}{r} 6 \\ +\,6 \\ \hline 12 \end{array} \qquad \begin{array}{r} 2 \\ +\,1 \\ \hline 3 \end{array} \qquad \begin{array}{r} 5 \\ +\,0 \\ \hline 5 \end{array}$$

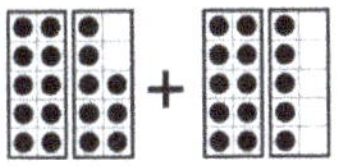

$$\begin{array}{r} 6 \\ +\,5 \\ \hline 11 \end{array} \qquad \begin{array}{r} 2 \\ +\,5 \\ \hline 7 \end{array} \qquad \begin{array}{r} 5 \\ +\,4 \\ \hline 9 \end{array} \qquad \begin{array}{r} 7 \\ +\,0 \\ \hline 7 \end{array}$$

$$\begin{array}{r} 9 \\ +\,7 \\ \hline 16 \end{array} \qquad \begin{array}{r} 9 \\ +\,3 \\ \hline 12 \end{array} \qquad \begin{array}{r} 2 \\ +\,4 \\ \hline 6 \end{array} \qquad \begin{array}{r} 5 \\ +\,6 \\ \hline 11 \end{array}$$

EXERCISE NO. 22

$$\begin{array}{r} 4 \\ +\,4 \\ \hline 8 \end{array} \qquad \begin{array}{r} 1 \\ +\,4 \\ \hline 5 \end{array} \qquad \begin{array}{r} 3 \\ +\,7 \\ \hline 10 \end{array} \qquad \begin{array}{r} 6 \\ +\,5 \\ \hline 11 \end{array}$$

$$\begin{array}{r} 2 \\ +\,4 \\ \hline 6 \end{array} \qquad \begin{array}{r} 9 \\ +\,0 \\ \hline 9 \end{array} \qquad \begin{array}{r} 1 \\ +\,3 \\ \hline 4 \end{array} \qquad \begin{array}{r} 6 \\ +\,0 \\ \hline 6 \end{array}$$

$$\begin{array}{r} 7 \\ +\,3 \\ \hline 10 \end{array} \qquad \begin{array}{r} 7 \\ +\,8 \\ \hline 15 \end{array} \qquad \begin{array}{r} 7 \\ +\,8 \\ \hline 15 \end{array} \qquad \begin{array}{r} 9 \\ +\,4 \\ \hline 13 \end{array}$$

6 +7 — 13	6 +2 — 8	3 +5 — 8	8 +8 — 16
3 +2 — 5	2 +8 — 10	3 +7 — 10	8 +3 — 11
9 +9 — 18	2 +0 — 2	9 +3 — 12	7 +3 — 10

1 +4 — 5	3 +7 — 10	7 +7 — 14	4 +3 — 7
8 +6 — 14	9 +5 — 14	9 +9 — 18	6 +5 — 11
8 +4 — 12	6 +6 — 12	5 +5 — 10	1 +9 — 10

3 +7 — 10	1 +0 — 1	6 +6 — 12	5 +7 — 12
7 +5 — 12	6 +4 — 10	2 +5 — 7	3 +2 — 5
5 +5 — 10	1 +8 — 9	7 +9 — 16	5 +5 — 10

4 +6 — 10	1 +1 — 2	5 +6 — 11	6 +5 — 11
6 +2 — 8	4 +3 — 7	6 +0 — 6	2 +5 — 7
9 +9 — 18	9 +6 — 15	6 +2 — 8	0 +4 — 4

| 8
+2
10 | 5
+6
11 | 1
+4
5 | 4
+8
12 |

| 1
+6
7 | 5
+9
14 | 2
+8
10 | 1
+7
8 |

| 9
+6
15 | 2
+8
10 | 1
+6
7 | 5
+5
10 |

| 12
+ 3
15 | 14
+ 8
22 | 16
+ 6
22 | 19
+ 9
28 |

| 14
+ 2
16 | 9
+ 6
15 | 18
+ 1
19 | 15
+ 9
24 |

| 13
+ 7
20 | 12
+ 4
16 | 16
+ 4
20 | 19
+ 1
20 |

| 14
+ 1
15 | 18
+ 5
23 | 17
+ 8
25 | 16
+ 7
23 |

| 12
+ 8
20 | 9
+ 4
13 | 17
+ 7
24 | 15
+ 3
18 |

| 19
+ 9
28 | 13
+ 1
14 | 18
+ 5
23 | 16
+ 6
22 |

| 9
+ 3
12 | 10
+ 7
17 | 11
+ 3
14 | 13
+ 8
21 |

| 14
+ 5
19 | 16
+ 2
18 | 15
+ 2
17 | 10
+ 9
19 |

| 12
+ 1
13 | 14
+ 6
20 | 17
+ 5
22 | 11
+ 1
12 |

| 9
+ 8
17 | 16
+ 7
23 | 10
+ 3
13 | 18
+ 6
24 |

| 19
+ 6
25 | 13
+ 1
14 | 15
+ 1
16 | 12
+ 5
17 |

| 14
+ 4
18 | 11
+ 3
14 | 14
+ 5
19 | 18
+ 2
20 |

| 18
+ 9
27 | 17
+ 3
20 | 16
+ 5
21 | 11
+ 4
15 |

| 13
+ 6
19 | 12
+ 5
17 | 16
+ 6
22 | 17
+ 4
21 |

| 13
+ 2
15 | 9
+ 1
10 | 11
+ 1
12 | 19
+ 2
21 |

| 16
+ 8
24 | 11
+ 6
17 | 13
+ 6
19 | 15
+ 1
16 |

| 19
+ 7
26 | 17
+ 7
24 | 9
+ 9
18 | 9
+ 4
13 |

| 12
+ 9
21 | 16
+ 8
24 | 10
+ 4
14 | 13
+ 3
16 |

| 9
+ 1
10 | 15
+ 1
16 | 16
+ 7
23 | 10
+ 7
17 |

| 17
+ 8
25 | 19
+ 3
22 | 12
+ 6
18 | 13
+ 4
17 |

| 17
+ 9
26 | 10
+ 5
15 | 12
+ 3
15 | 11
+ 5
16 |

```
  13      11      12       9
+  3    +  2    +  9     +  9
----    ----    ----     ----
  16      13      21      18

  15      10      16      17
+  7    +  4    +  5     +  4
----    ----    ----     ----
  22      14      21      21

  19      12      15      14
+  7    +  1    +  5     +  2
----    ----    ----     ----
  26      13      20      16
```



```
   9      17      15      17
+  9    +  9    +  2     +  4
----    ----    ----     ----
  18      26      17      21

  15      19      18      13
+  3    +  3    +  6     +  8
----    ----    ----     ----
  18      22      24      21

   9      16      11      13
+  2    +  5    +  7     +  1
----    ----    ----     ----
  11      21      18      14
```



```
  13      17       9       9
+  4    +  8    +  3     +  9
----    ----    ----     ----
  17      25      12      18

  18      14      10      19
+  8    +  2    +  4     +  7
----    ----    ----     ----
  26      16      14      26

  16      14      12      19
+  6    +  9    +  1     +  1
----    ----    ----     ----
  22      23      13      20
```



```
  13      11      10      17
+  9    +  4    +  1     +  8
----    ----    ----     ----
  22      15      11      25

  18      15       9      13
+  7    +  2    +  5     +  5
----    ----    ----     ----
  25      17      14      18

  19      12      12      18
+  3    +  6    +  7     +  1
----    ----    ----     ----
  22      18      19      19
```

20 + 11 31	11 + 15 26	18 + 20 38	12 + 16 28
15 + 13 28	19 + 15 34	17 + 14 31	15 + 10 25
18 + 14 32	12 + 12 24	14 + 13 27	17 + 11 28

17 + 18 35	18 + 20 38	15 + 14 29	18 + 16 34
15 + 13 28	11 + 16 27	17 + 17 34	14 + 10 24
13 + 15 28	10 + 17 27	13 + 19 32	20 + 20 40

14 + 11 25	10 + 10 20	12 + 11 23	19 + 13 32
18 + 12 30	15 + 20 35	11 + 19 30	13 + 15 28
10 + 16 26	17 + 14 31	16 + 14 30	20 + 17 37

17 + 13 30	13 + 12 25	11 + 19 30	10 + 19 29
16 + 13 29	20 + 10 30	11 + 18 29	12 + 17 29
20 + 10 30	19 + 11 30	18 + 17 35	17 + 16 33

19 + 10 29	12 + 13 25	10 + 12 22	14 + 19 33
13 + 15 28	18 + 16 34	20 + 14 34	17 + 15 32
15 + 13 28	19 + 10 29	18 + 20 38	12 + 17 29

20 + 18 38	13 + 20 33	12 + 20 32	17 + 14 31
16 + 17 33	13 + 13 26	10 + 13 23	18 + 12 30
10 + 16 26	14 + 10 24	19 + 19 38	15 + 12 27

14 + 10 24	15 + 19 34	10 + 14 24	14 + 20 34
16 + 17 33	19 + 18 37	17 + 14 31	16 + 16 32
15 + 12 27	10 + 10 20	13 + 17 30	19 + 13 32

17 + 12 29	13 + 13 26	15 + 20 35	11 + 18 29
18 + 16 34	14 + 11 25	15 + 17 32	12 + 11 23
17 + 13 30	12 + 10 22	11 + 15 26	10 + 19 29

Visit

BABY PROFESSOR
EDUCATION KIDS

www.BabyProfessorBooks.com
to download Free Baby Professor eBooks
and view our catalog of new and exciting
Children's Books